FOREWORD

Learning: a sense-maker's guide is a timely publication and an essential contribution to the debate about teaching and learning. As the title suggests, this book is not merely about making sense of learning. Importantly, it aims to help the reader to make critical sense of the plethora of new ideas about learning and to use what is available selectively and intelligently. It is a key part of ATL's *Teaching to Learn* campaign which aims to put learning at the centre of the education policy agenda.

When, well over a year ago, Chris Watkins was commissioned to write this publication, we chose an author who we knew to have extensive knowledge about learning and about learning to learn; the writing skills to communicate effectively with his audience; and the energy and enthusiasm to do the job really well. He was asked to:

- summarise the 'best' of what is known about learning

- look at ways in which what we *know* about learning may inform what teachers *do* about learning

- take a critical view of current offerings which claim to be about learning (for example brain-friendly learning, learning styles, brain gym, emotional intelligence, assessment for learning)

- provide signposts for readers who want to find out more.

We are delighted with the result.

This publication comes at a critical time. As this book goes to press, the Department for Education and Skills is about to launch a consultation on the core principles of teaching and learning. It is the intention that, once agreed, these principles will constitute the Department's expectations and guidance for schools. This is the first time that the State has become actively involved in establishing its own principles and expectations for pedagogy. Should we be pleased?

There are some who would hold fast to what is already enshrined in law and who would continue to argue that the State has no role in determining how things are taught in schools. Others might say that since the State has already been powerfully instrumental in influencing how things are taught (by, for example, introducing the national literacy and numeracy strategies and the Key Stage 3 National Strategy) the invitation to engage in a debate about first principles has come somewhat late in the day. The pragmatist might say that, like it or not, the State is now attempting to lead the debate on teaching and learning and it would be perverse not to engage in that debate with a view to influencing the final outcome. This is the view being taken by ATL.

Although written with practising teachers and lecturers in mind, *Learning: a sense-maker's guide* is a book which a wide range of readers will find of value: teaching assistants and others who work to support pupils' learning in schools and colleges; headteachers and governors; students of education and lecturers in higher education; and administrators and managers in local authorities. Politicians and policy-makers might learn a lesson or two as well.

Dr Mary Bousted
ATL General Secretary Elect
June 2003

WHY A GUIDE TO LEARNING?

The word 'learning' seems to be used more and more frequently nowadays, but on closer examination it is often the case that something else is being talked about. If we look closely at school life, it can be that there is very little talk of learning. There are many 'initiatives' which *claim* to be about learning, but their focus is somewhere else. A close look at some of these initiatives shows that they contribute little to learning and to improving education. In some cases new fads and fashions make things worse, not better.

Teachers may well find use for a guide which helps them make sense of all this – something which summarises what is known about learning in classrooms and schools and colleges and helps them position some of the initiatives which come their way.

This text is drawn from two important sources: voices from the varied literature and research on learning, and the voices of learners themselves – especially those in schools, whether they be pupils or teachers. By recognising how learning is being talked about around them, readers may be able more easily to navigate the terrain of learning in school life. This will not result in quick-fix add-ons for classroom life, but may well lead to more substantial change. By providing a brief guide to the hundreds of research studies which act as foundation for this text, readers may be also better equipped to critically assess the claims about learning which are made.

Teachers can play a key role in making real some of the rhetoric about a 'learning society'. We are living in a world where knowledge is expanding rapidly, and is no longer the province of a small elite. Every individual's learning landscape could become richer and more connected: learning can be recognised in every part of life, rather than it being merely the province of schools and colleges. Teachers, as professionals in learning, can make a vibrant contribution to such a life for young people and can act as formative guides to their lives of learning.

ABOUT THE AUTHOR

Chris Watkins is course tutor for the MA in Effective Learning at the University of London Institute of Education, a reader in education, having previously been a maths teacher in a large secondary school, a teacher in charge of a unit for pupils whose effect on school was sometimes disruptive, and a trained school counsellor.

Colleagues, co-authors, and co-learners in courses and projects have contributed immensely to this and other publications that he has been involved in. These include:

Learning and Leading
(2003, National College for School Leadership)

Effective Learning
(2002, National School Improvement Network with Eileen Carnell, Caroline Lodge, Patsy Wagner and Caroline Whalley)

Learning about Learning Enhances Performance
(2001, National School Improvement Network)

Learning about Learning
(2000, Routledge, with Eileen Carnell, Caroline Lodge, Patsy Wagner and Caroline Whalley)

Tomorrow's Schools – Towards Integrity
(2000, Routledge, edited with Ron Best and Caroline Lodge)

Improving School Behaviour
(2000, Paul Chapman Publishing, with Patsy Wagner)

Managing Classroom Behaviour
(1997, Association for Teachers and Lecturers).

CONTENTS

1 TALKING ABOUT LEARNING – ARE WE REALLY?

Have you noticed what can happen in conversations which aim to be about learning? They often slip into a conversation with a different focus. On those occasions, when we're trying to give some space to consider learning, various 'space invaders' take over the room. It's important we spot this, because we may need to keep them to one side for our discussion on learning. There are three main culprits.

1. TEACHING

In recent years, phrases such as 'teaching and learning policies' or 'teaching and learning strategies' have been used more and more. But close examination suggests that they might better read 'teaching and teaching', since the real attention given to learning is minimal. And the phrase is also often said as 'teaching'n'learning' – rather like 'fish'n'chips' – the 'and' is almost missed, whereas it represents both the challenge and achievement of the teaching profession. The links between teaching and learning are complex and multiple. High-level learning doesn't come from teachers teaching their socks off.

See what happens to your thinking when you tackle this question: *'Which do you think happens more often – teaching without learning or learning without teaching?'*.

2. PERFORMANCE

'Performance' is not learning, though it may develop from learning. Politicians and policy-makers have reduced the goal of schools and colleges to measurable outcomes of a limited sort: *performance* tables, *performance* pay, *performance* management. From the confines of their parallel universe, they create and disperse lists by which all shall be judged. In order to achieve compliance, a sprinkling of fear is added, and under such pressures there is a grave risk that teachers pass this on to pupils. The Prime Minister modelled this, saying *'We're putting the teaching profession under a lot of pressure, and we're doing it for a simple reason: there are a lot of people putting us under pressure'* (2 Feb 2002, Independent Radio News). Under conditions of pressure and compliance, some people talk about consistency as though it were a goal. Yet education cannot be about consistency: consistency means that you know tomorrow what you know today – and it could be consistently bad.

The distinction between learning and performance is crucial and will be addressed throughout this publication. Briefly, the evidence is that a focus on *performance* can depress performance: learners end up with negative ideas about their competence, they seek help less, use fewer strategies, and become organised by the very judgements which do them down. And the evidence is that a focus on *learning* can enhance performance.

3. WORK

Just listen in any classroom: *'Get on with your work'*, *'Home work'*, *'Schemes of work'*, *'Have you finished your work?'*. It's the dominant discourse of classroom life. But it can lead to a situation of meaningless work, as when people talk about being 'on task' without assessing the learning quality or engagement. The space invader of 'work' can be addressed quite effectively – especially with collaboration. Naheeda, teaching in Greenwich, agreed with her class that every time she and they seemed about to use the word 'work', they would try the word 'learning' instead. The effects were electric and led to much more engagement. Try it out.

 Do you recognise these three 'space invaders'? Are there others you would add to the list?

 Think for a moment about your experience of these 'space invaders'. How do they manage to take attention away from learning?

2 LEARNING – THREE MAIN VIEWS

When people talk or write about learning, they may adapt more simple or more complex views of what learning is. Their view of learning may take into account more elements or less elements, and these differences have considerable impact on how we think about any action which should follow – for example action to promote learning.

We can group views about learning into three broad groups, each of which takes a different stance on who is doing what to (or with) whom. Perhaps you notice examples of these three being used around you in your daily life. They also show up in how learners talk about learning. In the explanations which follow, some quotes from pupils (Year 7s unless otherwise stated) are included.

1. LEARNING IS BEING TAUGHT – LBT FOR SHORT

Put as simply as this, the first conception may seem daft, but look out – it's the dominant conception in our society. Deep-seated cultural beliefs hold that teaching is telling and learning is listening. Students repeat it, despite also saying how fragile it is.

'The best way I learn is by listening to the teacher but if there is noise around, the teacher's words just go through one ear and out the other' (Hamza)

Look at the way learning is portrayed in popular newspapers for examples of *learning is being taught* (LBT) – sometimes put in the voice of a parent. A school which chose not to use red pen when writing on pupils' work became newsworthy for example when parents were reported to have complained *'Don't bother about the colour of the ink: just tell them when they've got it wrong'.*

A slightly richer version of LBT holds that teaching is communicating thoughts in speech or writing. Learning is simply the reverse procedure – listening and reading. Nevertheless, the communication is conceived of as one-way, even by those with enthusiasm.

'I love to read to the class, I learn by listening to people' (Codi)

Many children (and quite a lot of adults) talk about their learning as LBT. Knowledge is somewhere 'out there', floating around in books or brains, and learning is about getting it into heads. This reflects another dominant image in our culture – that the mind is a container.

'I learn quickly and it stays in my head' (George)

Pupils are sometimes told that 'LBT' by sources in school, with associated ideas of good and bad learners and a view of knowledge as fixed and quantifiable 'things' to 'take in'.

'Mr M says a good learner knows he can only learn one or two things at a time and take them in fully, but a bad learner tries to learn a hundred things at once and doesn't take each thing in' (John, 14 years)

Much of the formal arrangement of schooling is built on the view that *learning is being taught.* As a teacher, you are regularly bombarded by it. The powers that be decide what should go into the child's mind (curriculum), hand that to teachers to 'deliver' (pedagogy) and then create tests to check that it's in there (assessment). In these processes, the child's mind is passive – a receptacle waiting to be filled – so the plans do not need to respond to the individuality of the learner or the contribution they make. Similarly, the teacher is a neutral conduit for the 'stuff' being delivered, and this again can be inspected without reference to the individuality of the teacher or the context of the school. Note that the evidence an Ofsted inspection seeks under the heading 'Quality of learning' is a 'response to teaching'. And the supposedly high-status institutions for learning in our society model this process: universities predominantly continue with lectures and lecturers.

Government uses of the term 'learning', although rare, usually embody the LBT view. For example, the Government website *Learndirect* is an information resource for choosing a course. And the engagingly-titled DfES booklets *Learning Journey* offer a description of subjects, tests, and so on, hardly using the word 'learn' after the booklet has been opened.

If learners vary in their learning, LBT has little constructive to say, since the learner is not its focus. If there is 'failure to learn', it is often attributed to the learner, but not in any sophisticated way, as for example when their 'ability' is invoked, or some unexplained mental ability (and there are plenty of these which have been invented). Learning deficit is some sort of a deficit in the learner – either in mental functioning or mental attitude (or having some barrier in your social background). The other alternative in this folk theory of one-way communication is that the teaching might be blamed – for example for not being 'clear' enough, or 'planned' enough, or 'structured' enough.

The academic perspective most associated with LBT is arguably behaviourism, a stance in psychology that studies only measurable behaviours. It does not conceive any internal processes of the learner, and the idea of the active mind is seen as a hindrance. It is also associated with seeing organisations as though they were machines, and embodies very dubious ethics in the power relations between teacher and taught.

In a view where learning is a passive process of knowledge acquisition, with predictable and measurable outcomes, perhaps the saddest aspect is its downplaying and discrediting the activity of the learner when describing learning and dishonouring their contribution to the process. Many adults, including teachers, report that it takes them many years after leaving school to become proactive learners.

2. LEARNING IS INDIVIDUAL SENSE-MAKING – LIS FOR SHORT

This second view focuses attention on the learner and their processes. It often highlights the processes which are called 'cognitive' (i.e. about thinking) but may also connect with emotional and social processes.

In this view, learning is the activity of the learner. S/he is active in constructing sense from the environment, not passively receiving it, and also active in that the particular sense made will reflect what s/he already knows and has experienced, as well as future goals and views of self.

'The way I learn is to work it out by myself' (Emily)

In *learning is individual sense-making* (LIS), the learner's mind is not seen as passive – and this contrast with LBT has a long history.

'The mind is not a vessel to be filled, but a fire to be ignited' (Plutarch, born 45 AD)

Learning is also described as an 'active' process in another sense – the active working with materials. This aspect is often reflected in the voice of learners themselves.

'I think that I am better at learning when I actually do things instead of just reading or writing something down' (Hannah)

'I think I'd learn a bit more if it was a bit more active' (Ben)

In LIS, the learner is not seen to discover an independent, pre-existing world outside the mind of the 'knower'. So distinctions such as 'objective *versus* subjective' are not used. Instead learners are involved in many two-way processes of inter-subjectivity: truths are the product of evidence, argument and construction. All the same, LIS often examines what is acquired through these processes, whether it is a conception, a notion, a misconception, a schema, or a mental representation. Thus it concurs with dictionary definitions of learning as 'the act of gaining knowledge', seeing it as an acquisition, like the accumulation of goods.

For LIS, the process of making sense of experience emphasises standing back from experience, so that reflection and review are important. The human capacity for thinking about thinking (meta-cognition) may be engaged, as well as the wider capacity for learning about learning (meta-learning). As will be seen in later sections of this book, what learners say to themselves about their own learning is important, and learners may offer contrasting views with contrasting approaches to learning-related activities.

'I keep my book neat. I do every homework that is set and bring it on time' (Kristina) contrasts with *'I enjoy making mistakes and learning from them'* (Harry).

If learning is individual sense-making, and the way in which learners make sense of their learning is also important, then it is important to focus on the way in which learners can take charge of their learning and handle it actively. The qualities of a self-directed learner become highlighted.

Much has been written on how the principles of LIS may be built into the practices of education, and it is also clear that many teachers who do so find themselves in tension with the cultural beliefs and practices summarised in the first view, LBT. For the teacher's role to become more that of 'guide on the side', rather than 'sage on the stage', we need to refocus attention from teacher to learner. As one major exponent puts it:

'What's the best way to improve teaching? Focus on learning. And the best way to increase learning? Move the focus off the teacher and onto the student' (David Kolb)

In order to make this change some key insights may help:

'The student knows more than the teacher about what he has learned – even if he knows less about what was taught' (Peter Elbow).

Critics of LIS, many of whom are (knowingly or not) proponents of LBT, try to discredit LIS as 'new-fangled' or 'modern'. However the change of emphasis was employed by Socrates (470-399 BC) who engaged his learners by asking questions. He often insisted that he really knew nothing, but his questioning skills allowed others to learn by self-generated understanding. Does this sound like your experience as a teacher when you help a pupil making sense? In the wider classroom context, the change of emphasis can also be read in the words of the person who is sometimes attributed with the foundation of a professional stance on teaching (didactics) and the invention of the school textbook for children.

'Let the beginning and the end of our didactics be: seek and find the methods where the teacher teaches less but they who sit in the desks, learn more. Let schools have less rush, less antipathy and less vain effort, but more well-being, convenience and permanent gain' (Jan Amos Comenius, 1632)

If learning is an individual making sense of experience, it is sometimes portrayed as a cycle in which all phases are necessary: an action experience, a reflection, a making sense and an application.

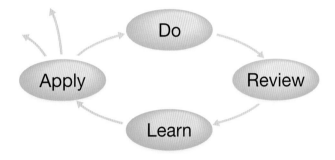

Thus a learning deficit might be understood as a lack of:

- particular experiences

- adopting a reflective stance to experience

- particular thinking for understanding

- future context for the learning to be applied.

How learning informs action in future situations is vital: LIS helps us see that learning is influenced by the use to which it is to be put. Some of the more linear practices in schools and colleges highlight application as a stage after understanding, but it is a hazard to separate them too much.

'We do not understand and then use, but we understand as we use and we use as we come to understand. The process of constructing understanding is thus, not only circular, but also endless' (Antonio Bettencourt)

Within LIS, a key strategy for enhancing learning is to ask learners to 'explain to themselves'. Young people recognise this in their view of learning, and may also foresee the process of explaining to others.

'I like learning more because I could explain some things more' (Jacob)

'I could learn something and then put it in my own words' (Bianca)

As a teacher you might recognise much of LIS in the processes you are aware of your pupils going through, but do you also recognise similar sense-making in yourself? And are you an individual who has made sense of your own learning? Or are you more like the senior teacher who said *'I've just realised that I went through the whole of my school career and noticed nothing about my learning'*?

3. LEARNING IS BUILDING KNOWLEDGE AS PART OF DOING THINGS WITH OTHERS – LBKO FOR SHORT

'Learning is cooperating' (Tom, 5 years)

This view develops the point that meaning is constructed together in social activity, not individually in people's heads. Human learning is necessarily and fundamentally social: it utilises language, culture and communication, and implicates our identities and preferred futures. All of these are social creations and are being dynamically re-created. We build our identities and connections around our work, knowledge, and contributions to our communities. Yet, sadly, schools and colleges often behave as if the social were a threat to learning, or think it should be addressed in a low-status corner of the curriculum.

Learning is building knowledge as part of doing things with others (LBKO) highlights the understanding that new knowledge emerges in the process of social activity and especially in dialogue. As a teacher you have doubtless had many occasions when you say something new to someone in a conversation, and think about it more later, perhaps relating it to other things you have said. This point has been made by theorists, ranging from Vygotsky to Annie.

'You learn more because if you explain to people what to do you say things that you wouldn't say to yourself, really. So you learn things that you wouldn't know if you were just doing it by yourself' (Annie)

LBKO draws our attention to the processes through which learners act as partners, communicate in relation to their activity, involve themselves in dialogue, and create a joint product which is more than the sum of the parts.

'I learn best working with a friend, they can explain it to me without me even asking. We can work together whilst combining answers' (Sarah-Jane)

'Your partner sitting next to you says something that you don't know and you say something that your partner doesn't know, then you will both learn something' (Usha, 8 years)

This view of learning sheds light on a wide range of communities of learners, ranging from those organisations (often in fast-moving industries) which come to be called learning organisations, to scientific communities, to jazz bands and to photocopier mechanics who never open the manual to fix a machine but who spend time talking with each other to do so. In all of these, the knowledge created, the activity, and the social relations are closely intertwined. As people are engaged together, they are also empowered – both to contribute and to influence. This view helps us see that the settings and situations which provide the most potential for learning are those in which participants are engaged in real action that has consequences not only for them but for their community as a whole.

In LBKO, the motivation to learn is linked to motivation for engagement, and the wish to enter and participate in new communities. It is this need for meaningful participation that may be similar for a gang member, a prize student, a scientist, a soloist, a public servant or an entrepreneur. Pupils often remark on their social motivation to create together.

'I find it hard to work all on my own some times so me and my partner give each other ideas' (Rhea)

Learning is the means by which people gain membership and participate in community activity, and so a 'failure' to learn is the result of exclusion from this participation. People have difficulty learning when they are marginal in a community.

When people have experienced learning as a community, their way of talking about their own learning may reflect this, as shown in this comment from a pupil in Juliet Bodger's Year 6 class:

'I think learning is… you watch, and you teach yourself sometimes or other people or other objects help you, and you… listen, you watch, and you add to what people say'.

Formal arrangements of schooling sometimes reflect LBKO, for example in a classroom where participants are working to create new and shared knowledge on an agreed focus. But these examples are in the minority. Outside school, this view of learning is more prevalent. Ninety per cent of all adults each year involve themselves in intentional learning projects, 75 per cent outside of institutional frameworks, and this 'informal' learning is a very social phenomenon with a lot of human interaction.

In LBKO the impact of culture is taken seriously, sometimes highlighting that we are all surrounded by the cultural objects in which meaning has been vested by previous generations, and (as anthropologists remind us) cultural and cognitive development constantly interact. Here the context in which meaning-making happens comes to be more important: more attention is paid to the processes by which learning communities are built.

As a teacher, you may see yourself as a leader of a community – LBKO would suggest as one of the leaders, for just as knowledge is distributed around persons, so is leadership. Such a person will be helping learners engage in 'generative' rather than 'passive' learning activities, and will act on the assumption that learners need to engage in collaborative argumentation and knowledge-testing. LBKO moves us from viewing learning as an acquisition, whatever the commodity to be acquired, towards viewing learning as becoming part of a community. A hazard of this view would be to to focus solely on social processes to the point of excluding individual ones.

What views of learning do you notice?
It is useful to notice two further ways in which the three views of learning differ: their complexity and their dominance. As we move through the three views, more elements are brought into the picture and more relations are implied in the way we talk about learning. A simple phrase for each shows that the subject and the verb change:

1. *S/he taught me…*

2. *I made sense…*

3. *We worked out that…*

Second, as we move though the three views, we move from the ones which are dominant in our culture (LBT) to those which are less dominant and less developed in our everyday language (LBKO). Realising this helps us to explain why the latter two are less evident in many classrooms: the practices which they require are not so practised and do not conform to some of the dominant cultural images of how teaching is seen – as transmission.

The three stances on learning do not come to life in neat, separate ways. Real life (and classroom life!) is a dynamic mixture, in which elements of all three may be present all the time. Use the framework opposite to help you capture what you notice around you, by noting examples and the relative balance of these views in how people talk, and in classroom and school practices.

	What people do, what people say
LBT 1 *S/he taught me…*	
LIS 2 *I made sense…*	
LBKO 3 *We worked out that…*	

Tensions between these three views can create tensions for us as educators. The way we have come to resolve these tensions is reflected in our answers to these questions:

- does learners' knowledge come from my transmission or their construction?

- is my job to deliver or to create an environment for seeking knowledge?

- does my teaching reflect policy or what I know about the learners?

- does my teaching make a difference or not?

- do I have the skills, or do I need to learn continuously?

- am I on my own, or do my context and colleagues matter?

As teachers, our particular resolutions to these tensions will reflect our vision of teaching, the features of the local context, how the political and cultural influences are responded to, and so on. In the last two decades, policy-makers have taken a concerted stance on these matters, through a welter of policies/initiatives/strategies based on 'LBT' and claiming 'to restore the true purpose of education based on the transmission of knowledge' and promoting 'the traditional teaching of literacy and numeracy' (Woodhead, 2001).

How have your views of learning been influenced by Government policies and by the dominant cultural beliefs on teaching and learning? How have you maintained your beliefs in the face of these influences?

3 BRAINS, INTELLIGENCES, STYLES – OR LEARNERS' ORIENTATIONS?

Recent years have seen many books, courses and packages which call on such terms as 'brain-friendly schooling', 'emotional intelligence', 'learning style' and so on. Where would we place such contributions on our emerging map of learning?

Stuff on brains (stuff in brains?)

Brains are often mentioned in relation to learning nowadays, with claims of how brain research informs the work of educators. Packages on sale in high street shops claim that they use findings from brain research to help people 'learn faster' and 'improve their memories'. But what view of learning are these products based on – 'getting things in your head'? That view of learning, although common, has little research evidence to support it. It's a part of 'LBT', and these folk theories do not maintain themselves by evidence. In everyday talk, people describe the brain as though it was a container, a repository of knowledge, but the evidence on brain functioning shows that it can't be like that. There is no one 'place' where 'information is stored'. Rather the brain is engaged in continuous, very flexible processing. Memories are not stored: they are always being constructed, refreshed and reconstructed. The most striking thing about the brain is its flexibility.

Popular views of brain research use simplifications which have been discredited by neuroscientists. For example the popular 'left brain-right brain' distinction is too simple – the evidence is that anything meaningful uses parts of both sides. Some neuroscientists conclude that any model that assigns collections of mental processes, such as spatial reasoning, to one hemisphere or the other is too crude to be useful. Similarly, in research of gender differences, most results are equivocal and there is little agreement as to what any identified differences mean.

Brain studies can measure brain activity, but this is not consciousness, even less learning. They can describe what occurs when someone is having an MRI scan, but not what happens when they are elsewhere. Given current understanding of learning and the key role of context, this is a fundamental weakness. Those who study memory and remembering say 'context is all' to remind us that this is not a matter of what is contained in our brains, but more a matter of what story we are able to tell, supported by the context we're in. We know that people learn very differently in different contexts, and that the landscape of learning is more expanded now than we used to consider it to be.

Some of the foremost neuroscientists are the first to admit that their findings have little direct application to education practice. Other analysts conclude that current brain research has little to offer educational practice or policy. So it is important to separate the science from the speculation. Some books which claim to be based on brain research propose educational practices which are based in long-standing theories of teaching and learning. As such they may reflect modern evidence on learning. But others reflect the restricted view (LBT), now with some 'go-faster' techniques for the learner. Such a limited conception is unlikely to transform learning: if it does not address the classroom it is not likely to improve classroom culture.

The same may be said for classroom activities such as 'brain gym'. Invented by a biology teacher, exercises which stimulate bodily activity may indeed have stimulating effects on the brain. But this is not learning, and even when it is claimed to be a preparation for learning, it is important to consider what sort of learning is to follow. At worst brain gym could provide a brief episode of bodily activity to precede a longer episode of learner passivity.

There is a hazard associated with focusing too much on brains: it could encourage crude views of some people being 'more brainy' than others, and could support too much of a biological view of human behaviour.

'I think that I'm quite a good learner but not that brainy' (Sanam)

We need to focus on meaning in learning: after all, memorisation is something we resort to when what we are learning does not make sense to us.

Intelligences

Intelligence is a term used more in USA than in UK, and it is from there that most of the attempts to revive and recycle the term have come: 'emotional intelligence', 'multiple intelligences', and so on. Again, the hazard is to encourage crude views of some learners being more 'intelligent' than others. The evidence does not support this: there is no connection between measured 'intelligence' (i.e. the ability to solve abstract problems that bear no relation to your goals under time pressure) and the higher-level skills and processes of an effective learner. However, the strength of the idea of multiple intelligences is the idea of multiplicity rather than the idea of intelligence. Anything which helps us as educators see more of the diversity in learners and the diversity in successful learning is to be welcomed. If the idea helps teachers recognise a wider range and cater for it in the classroom, it is of benefit, even though it has taken our attention (once again) from learning to teaching.

Learning styles

Sometimes in schools and colleges there is a tendency to put young people into this category or that, but the effects are at times unfortunate. 'Style' is a fashionable label and it has become fashionable in some quarters to apply labels to learners. There are a number of different versions of 'learning style' being promulgated, and they have little in common. It therefore becomes important to ask 'what view of learning is this based on?' Some are about preferences for the 'intake of information', yet this notion of learning has long been seen as erroneous. Other versions of 'learning style' are supposedly about consistent tendencies, rather like personality, but a person's approach to learning varies across situations – and it should, in order to be effective. It has also become popular to say that learning is more effective when learners 'match' their style with the context, yet there is equal evidence to support the idea that learning is more effective where there is a mismatch. If our aim is to support learners in becoming self-directed, then they need to be equipped with a full range of styles. A hazard in current times is when the notion of style leads learners to categorise themselves in a fixed language: for example 'I'm a visual learner'. This could link to a less versatile approach to learning.

But learners do vary – all of us do. Sometimes according to our purpose, or the context we are in, or other factors. So what long-standing and dependable evidence is there regarding such variation?

Learners' orientations to learning

Over a number of decades, in a number of countries, with learners ranging from four-year-olds to Olympic athletes, research has highlighted an important way in which we can all differ as learners.

Learning orientation	Performance orientation
We believe that effort can lead to success	We believe that ability leads to success (and you have it or you don't)
We believe in our ability to improve and learn, and not be fixed or stuck	We are concerned to be seen as able, and to perform well in others' eyes
We prefer challenging tasks, whose outcome reflects our approach	We seek satisfaction from doing better than others
We get satisfaction from our own personally-defined successes at difficult tasks	We emphasise competition, public evaluation
We talk to ourselves: when engaged in a task we talk ourselves through	When the task is difficult we display helplessness: 'I can't do X'

It is best not to think of these orientations as simply describing different learners. Even though learners may be more dominated by one than the other, we can all adopt these orientations, depending on the context.

 Do you know of learners who (in the context that you meet them) display more learning orientation, and others that display more performance orientation?

'I like challenging and new things to learn and even though sometimes I don't get it I'll ask' (Christopher)

The difference can be summed up as:

A concern for improving one's competence	A concern for proving one's competence

Now here's the important point: a learning orientation gets you better performance, while a performance orientation can lower performance. Here's an 11-year-old who says it clearly:

'The way I learn helps me get high scores. I revise on tests that's why I scored 86 per cent in science' (Jai)

Learners with a performance orientation display negative effects:

- greater helplessness – 'I'm no good at X'

- they seek help less (from peers or teachers)

- they use less strategies

- they continue to use strategies which aren't effective

- they have a greater focus on grades, not process.

All of these are associated with worse performance.

It can be useful for teachers and pupils to discuss learning orientation and performance orientation. Sometimes a survey of views could contribute to the discussion (and set a baseline for development of more learning orientation). A brief enquiry format is given below.

We're interested in your views about your learning. There aren't any 'right' or 'wrong' answers. Can you tell us how you approach your learning? Just put a tick in the column on the right, to show whether you:

		Strongly agree	Agree	Disagree	Strongly disagree
1	I like school work that I'll learn from, even if I make a lot of mistakes				
2	I'd feel really good if I were the only one who could answer questions in class				
3	An important reason why I do my school work is because I like to learn new things				
4	It's very important to me that I don't look stupid in class				
5	I like school work best when it really makes me think				
6	It's important that other students in my class think that I'm good at my work				
7	An important reason why I do my work in school is I want to get better at it				
8	An important reason I do my school work is so that I don't embarrass myself				
9	I do my school work because I'm interested in it				
10	I want to do better than other students in my classes				
11	An important reason I do my school work is because I enjoy it				
12	The reason I do my work is so others won't think I'm dumb				

4 LEARNING GOALS IN CLASSROOMS

In recent years, there has developed a practice of displaying 'learning objectives' on the classroom wall. These are, of course, teaching objectives. Sometimes they might be the teacher's objectives but they are mostly cast in the language of curriculum planners.

There are two impacts of this practice which should concern us: pupils get bored with it (and some teachers too!), and it leads to a narrowing of the purposes in classrooms, as indicated by Kieran, a Year 6 teacher who said: *'Do you know what I've found myself doing of late? When pupils ask "Why are we doing this?", I've been replying "Because it's in the SATs"'*. His sense of surprise at himself was clear as he spoke.

It doesn't have to be like that.

If you do display these official statements:

- help the learners make their own sense of them: for example give them two minutes in pairs to discuss what these statements might mean.

- help the learners make them useful: give them two minutes to discuss *'If someone had learned this, how could they make use of it?'.*

While you might predict that they will have little to say, you are likely to be surprised.

These official statements are one part of a wider range of statements you can hear in a classroom, all of which provide purposes for learning. These statements may emerge when someone asks you *'What's the point of this?'* and on other occasions. They vary in important ways and can have significant effects on the 'motivational climate' for learning in a classroom.

Think about the statements in your classroom which bring purpose to learning. What would be the overall balance in the four sorts shown in the framework opposite?

'Do it for me' 'Do it because it's in the test' 'Do it to avoid detention' (Internal to the classroom, but external to the learner)	'Do it for your parents' 'Do it for your success in later life' 'Do it for the school' (External to the classroom, and external to the learner)
'Do it because it's interesting' 'Do it because you'll learn' 'Do it to contribute to all our learning' (Internal to the classroom, and internal to the learner)	'Do it because you can use it' 'Do it to find out about the world' 'Do it to improve things' (External to the classroom, but internal to the learner)

If we do not use the bottom half of this framework we are unlikely to be promoting self-directing and effective learners. If we do not use purpose statements like those in the bottom left quadrant, we may not find learners maximally engaged. Learning is an end in itself, and any task, no matter how enjoyable it once seemed, can be devalued if presented as a means rather than an end.

THE SELF-DIRECTED LEARNER

Teachers often say that they wish their pupils were more responsible. But this can turn into a moral complaint rather than a plan for improvement. If we want to understand and develop more self-directed learners, it's most productive to focus on what such a learner can do.

1. AT A MINIMUM, SELF-DIRECTED LEARNERS CAN:

- focus on a given activity

- manage distractions

- organise information they are given

- focus on teachers and what they are saying.

But this is all from a compliance view of learning – learning as being taught (LBT).

'I'm smart if I focus' (Curtis)

2. WITH SUPPORT, SELF-DIRECTED LEARNERS CAN:

- generate their own inquiries

- plan how they'll go about an activity (including activities such as reading and writing)

- monitor how well an activity is going

- review whether the strategies they have used have proved effective.

The process for these activities to occur can be individual learners generating their own questions before, during and after an activity. It reflects the view of learning as individual sense-making (LIS).

'When I'm stuck, I go back and check instead of guessing' (Vikesh)

'I am good at finding short cuts and providing tactical tips' (Daniel)

3. AT BEST, SELF-DIRECTED LEARNERS CAN:

- select from their environment appropriate resources they need for learning (peers, teachers, other resources)

- generate with others motivation and goals

- promote and develop with others dialogue for learning

- inter-relate learning from various contexts of their learning landscapes.

The process for these activities to develop is relatively rare in our schools and colleges: it is the promotion of classrooms as learning communities (LBKO).

 How do you regard yourself as a learner on the three aspects of self-regulated learning listed on this page? And how does your answer reflect your experiences of learning and your career as a learner?

When teachers think about pupils, they often under-estimate pupils' processes of self-regulation, perhaps because these processes are not easily visible. The results of talking to pupils about their self-regulation in learning paints a different picture. Pupils give increased reports of their self-regulation, and seek more.

'[Our teacher] doesn't exactly tell us the answer, otherwise we wouldn't learn anything (Aysha, 8 years)

Talking about this theme can be initiated in many ways. At most simple, try asking a class *'Who's in charge of your learning?'* In many contexts, you will hear the reply *'teachers',* and if you wait for more alternative answers you may wait a while before they add themselves to the list.

Sometimes a survey of views could contribute to the discussion (and set a baseline for development of more self-regulated learning). A brief enquiry format follows.

We're interested in your views about your learning. There aren't any 'right' or 'wrong' answers. Can you tell us how much you feel you're in charge of your learning? Just put a tick in the column on the right, to show your opinion:

		Strongly agree	Agree	Disagree	Strongly disagree
1	Before I start my work, I work out the best way to do it				
2	I can do my best even if I don't like what the lesson is about				
3	When my teacher gives hints on how best to do something, I'll try them out				
4	I sometimes ask myself 'Am I going about this the best way?'				
5	I know when I've understood something when I can say it in my own words				
6	If I find something difficult in class, I talk to the teacher				
7	I don't ask questions in class				
8	When I'm reading I sometimes stop to make sure I'm understanding				
9	With a new topic I can usually find something interesting to learn				
10	When I get new work, I jump straight in and sometimes wish I hadn't				
11	When I don't understand something in a lesson, I ask a classmate				

Note that if a 'score' were to be derived from responses to these items, numbers 7 and 10 would need to be reverse-scored.

PROMOTING SELF-DIRECTED LEARNERS IN CLASSROOMS AND SCHOOL

 Is there any point in developing self-directed learners, especially when teachers have been landed with the responsibility for learners' performance? Yes, even for the performance pressures of current times, those pupils who plan and reflect get significantly better marks in GCSE, and they achieve this in collaborative classrooms. More long-term, if young people are to make the most of themselves in a fast-changing world, their competence in this area is vital.

In classrooms which promotes self-directed learners, pupils are:

- making choices – of activities, within activities, when an activity is completed

- making goals their own

- involved in planning how they will proceed

- given encouragement to offer commentary on their learning – talking aloud

- supported in reviewing their experience – telling the story

- evaluating the end-product

- asking others for help

- motivated by internal incentives.

As discussed previously, learners who are self-directed are also those who show a learning orientation. They are more effective learners for many other contexts of life.

But how do we make sense of 'effective learning' and 'effective learners'?

Think of a particular learner who (as far as you are able to tell) seems to be an effective learner.

What can you see/hear that learner doing/saying which links to the fact that you think they are an effective learner? [Note that you are being asked to think about what that learner says or does – this is to take the focus away from hypothetical ideas like 'motivation' and towards practical actions like 'shows interest'.]

This reflection regularly leads teachers to identify areas such as:

- making connections (between experiences, ideas, people, contexts)

- using a range of sources and resources: people

- offering a commentary on the process of learning

- being able to plan, review, change strategy etc

- demonstrating curiosity and risk-taking.

Such qualities are rarely given explicit support or development in many aspects of school life, yet they are core features of what is understood to be an effective learner.

The word 'effective' is rarely defined, despite being used frequently. In order to define it we need to recognise the context and the goals: effective for when? Effective for what?

In current times:

- the knowledge base in society is increasing rapidly, and now doubles every 373 days – teaching knowledge is an anachronism

- a wider range of the population process and generate knowledge – information is not the possession of a few 'experts'

- employment prospects relate more to the ability to enhance and transfer learning – the accumulation of qualifications is not enough

- the landscape of learning is much wider and richer, involving multiple contexts, modes and sources – learning is no longer the province of special institutions: it is a way of being.

In such a context, the goals of learning need to focus less on 'acquiring knowledge', and more on generating knowledge with others – less of LBT, and more of LBKO.

Effective learners have learned how to become effective learners. This involves not just the acquisition of strategies, but the monitoring and reviewing of learning to see whether particular strategies are effective. No one strategy works for all goals and purposes (although some of them are sold as though this was the case!).

Learning is:

- an activity of construction, not one of reception

- handled with others, or (even when alone) in the context of others

- driven by learner's agency (intentions and choices).

Effective learning is all of these at their best, *plus* the monitoring and review of whether approaches and strategies are proving effective for the particular goals and context.

 How can you help learners become more effective at checking whether their strategies are effective?

EFFECTIVE LEARNING IN CLASSROOMS

The typical classroom is not necessarily the best-designed environment for what we now know about learning. The busy, public, multi-dimensional nature of classroom life makes it the most complex environment on the planet. Classrooms sometimes seem to develop a life of their own in which learning is a neglected focus. Yet, against the odds, there are times when effective learning occurs in that context. What can we learn from the best of those times?

Take a few minutes to think of a classroom you know, in which the sense of learning has been really positive. Maybe there has been engagement, excitement, reflection, and so on.

Choose the best experience you can. When you have identified that situation, do all you can to reconstruct it in your mind's eye – recall the room, the conditions, the people and so on. Capture in concrete detail the things that made that experience possible.

Now ask yourself: *What was positive about the learning?*

How do you make sense of this positive occasion, how was it made possible?

Try to capture some of what you have identified into a provocative proposition about this classroom: *'To me, effective learning happens when…'*

The themes which emerge from this 'appreciative inquiry' relate closely to those listed in the table below.

Of the four items in the table, the first three could be found in reviews of effective classroom learning half a century ago. The fourth, learning about learning, is one of the crucial additions for our developing understanding of learning in the changing world.

If effective learning is:	then promoting effective learning involves:
an activity of construction (i.e. making meaning not receiving)	action and reflection (i.e. using materials and creating ideas)
handled with, or in the context of, others (even when alone, others are influential)	collaboration (in order that dialogue occurs)
driven by learners' agencies (their sense of intention and choice)	learner responsibility (so that planning is involved)
involving monitoring and review (especially of the learning process),	learning about learning (to notice and improve the process).

8 TEACHING FOR LEARNING

This simple phrase sounds at first as though it would describe all teaching, but it denotes a significant change of emphasis from the dominant patterns of classroom life. It marks the idea that teachers focus on what the learners are doing rather than what they the teachers are doing. This is the focus which is adopted by many effective and many experienced teachers.

When planning teaching for learning, our task as teachers is to focus on the experience for learners, rather on what we are going to say and do. We need to consider the experiences pupils will have and the ways we will support them to learn from those experiences. A model (shown opposite) of the phases that the learner goes through may help.

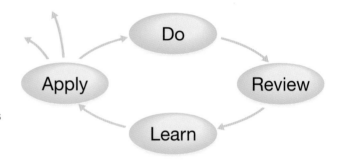

These four phases may be planned on each of the aspects which promote effective learning. The whole picture is shown in the matrix below.

		Active learning	Collaborative Learning	Learner responsibility	Learning about learning
	Do	Tasks are designed for learner activity, using or creating materials, texts, performances	Tasks in small groups connect to create a larger whole (by roles or by parts)	Learners exercise choice and plan their approaches	Learners are encouraged to notice aspects of their learning as they engage in tasks
	Review	Learners stop to notice what happened, what was important, how it felt, etc.	Learners bring ideas together and review how the group has operated	Learners monitor their progress and review their plans	Learners describe what they notice and review their learning (goals, strategies, feelings, outcomes, context)
	Learn	New insights and understandings are made explicit	Explanations of topic and of how the group functioned are voiced across the group	Factors affecting progress are identified and new strategies devised	Richer conceptions of learning are voiced and further reflective inquiry is encouraged
	Apply	Future action is planned in light of new understanding. Transferring that understanding to other situations is examined	Future possibilities for group and community learning are considered	Plans are revised to accommodate recent learning	Learners plan to notice more and to experiment with their approaches to learning

Consider a classroom activity that you have planned or are about to plan. Are there extra elements which this grid brings to your attention that you would like to include in your planning?

 Consider some ways in which you could use these ideas for other aspects of your teaching, and/or share them with a colleague.

Deciding where to start

When making changes in classroom life, it might help to select a manageable focus.

 Select a classroom you know well, and where you think that the quality of learning could be improved.

Think of the overall profile of activities for pupils in this classroom for, say, half a term.

On the scale below, give a quick indication of the extent to which the profile of activities in the classroom could be described by each of the headings.

	Very little	Somewhat	Quite a lot	A lot
Active learning (not merely 'activity')				
Collaborative learning (not merely 'discussing')				
Learner responsibility (for matters in learning)				
Learning about learning (strategies and reflection)				

 If effective learning is promoted through these four:

a. which of the four would you choose as a priority for development in this classroom?

b. which of the four do you think you are likely to experiment with?

c. which of the four would you wish to know more about?

9 HELPING LEARNERS MAKE SENSE OF THEIR LEARNING

All too often, children are treated as though they have nothing worthwhile to say about how their learning happens. The dominant pattern is not to engage learners' voices on learning, missing a key opportunity for them to come to understand their learning. Teachers may once have been treated like this when they were at school.

Making sense of learning has parallels with how we make sense of other things: we do it gradually, we do it by focusing on experiences and trying out explanations. Our knowledge and language build as we go, yet also remain somewhat fragmented and partial.

There are four broad sorts of classroom practices which help learners make sense of their learning, and these have been developed with all ages, from four years upward. They build on each other and lead to a key ingredient in effective learning – one which also is reflected in improved performance.

FIRST PRACTICE: NOTICING LEARNING

This requires that we occasionally *stop the flow* of classroom life and activity in order to notice. Notice what we did, what the effects were, how it felt, what helped, how we persevered, what we thought we might do with the learning. In these moments we highlight experiences needed to build up a language for noticing learning.

SECOND PRACTICE: CONVERSATIONS ABOUT LEARNING

This can start with pupils discussing in pairs what they have noticed, or with teacher prompts which help learners reflect on why they were doing certain things which are normally taken for granted: *'How come that we [did X] yesterday?' 'Did you find out anything new?' 'How?' 'How could you find out more?'*

THIRD PRACTICE: REFLECTION

Reflection can be supported, for example, by writing in a 'learning log' – a notebook or other format for jotting down noticings and thoughts, sometimes with the help of specific prompts from teacher.

'These log entries help me a lot. As I write I notice and understand more too' (Lynne, 10 years)

'It's only when you start to write these things down that you think, "Well I could do something about that"' (Robert)

FOURTH PRACTICE: MAKING LEARNING AN OBJECT OF LEARNING

When learning can be talked about in some detail, can be reviewed, and described more richly, explicit experiments can be set up to adapt some part of it. It can be done in any context, any classroom, by adding a cycle of learning about learning to the cycle of learning about 'content'. For example on one occasion we might review, examine and experiment with how we went about reading. It might be that this highlighted the goals we have in mind for our learning, so that they could be examined on another occasion. Or we could look at how we handled feelings. Or how we engaged others and how best they help. Features of the context could be reviewed and improved. And so on.

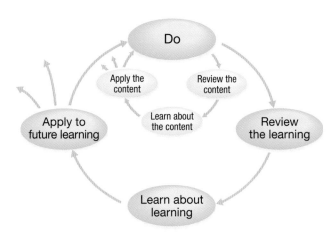

10 THINKING SKILLS?

The idea of 'thinking skills' attracts a burst of interest approximately each decade – usually as a response to the recognition that force-feeding facts with a fire-hose is not working, and there is a need for something 'higher order'.

A similar phenomenon has occurred in USA, where thinkers on learning have concluded:

- thinking isn't really a 'higher-order' activity – thinking is a part of learning everything

- thinking isn't really a 'skill' – we can't take thinking out of thinking about something, and learning to think can't be tacked on to an otherwise business-as-usual programme of instruction

- thinking can't be divided into convenient components for teaching and testing – if you analyse thinking into tiny bits and then teach those bits, you get many little bits that never get put together and that probably can't be put together (this explains why students who are trained in all kinds of separate thinking skills don't usually think better as a result)

- thinking depends on context – abilities learned in one place can't be lifted out of context and used somewhere else, and we need to make learning in school a lot more like the learning in other contexts that students are preparing for.

None of this is to suggest that we do not want to support young people in thinking well – it is more an issue of how to go about supporting them. Many of the approaches which have led into the development of 'skills packages' have an underlying view of pupils' deficit. The many and varied lists of thinking skills carry the message that pupils can't do them so we must teach them. This stance risks ignoring that they may be thinking well in other contexts. An approach which avoids this trap uses 'infusion', where contexts for developing thinking are identified in classroom and curriculum, and then lessons are planned where thinking and topic understanding can be explicitly and simultaneously pursued. In this:

- thinking is seen as a 'hidden skill' needing to be made explicit through discussion, reflection and collaborative enquiry

- pupils must be given the time and opportunity to talk about thinking processes

- an important aim is to develop a language for talking about thinking, to make steps more explicit and transparent (for both pupils and teachers), and to slow down the thinking process so that pupils have time to grasp what might be involved.

The approach represents a shift to a thinking curriculum, thinking classrooms and schools for thought, in other words supporting teaching for thoughtfulness.

THINKING-CENTRED LEARNING

The approach considered in the previous section promotes 'thinking-centred learning', which can happen through:

- emphasis on pupils explaining – to self and to others

- classroom discussion around thought-demanding questions, and pupils' questions *('Can something be destroyed or just changed?' 'How do wars start?'* (Bill, 9 years))

- use of authentic problems that have real-world significance

- peer teaching, where pupils must think through a topic carefully in order to teach it to other pupils

- problem-based learning, where pupils study content by learning to solve problems

- project-based learning, where pupils gain content knowledge through complex, often socially meaningful projects

- engagement in 'performances of understanding' which ask pupils to demonstrate their understanding

- critical and creative thinking infused into learning a subject, where pupils analyse, critique, defend, ask 'what-if' questions, and explore alternative points of view.

12 LEARNING AND CONTEXT

Think of your own experiences of learning, in any of the contexts of your life – employment, home, play or hobbies or sport (or even when you were a pupil at school!). As you compare your own experiences of learning in those different contexts, what do you notice? Does your learning relate to the place, the company, the purpose? Do all of these influence the activity you were involved in, your relations with other people and the way you go about your learning?

Many adults are active, self-directed learners and they want to learn! Adults' intentional learning projects are mostly self-guided and outside of institutional frameworks: they centre around self-motivated and self-directed learning, which is integral to life. They are characterised by the learner controlling the learning process.

Many people find that their experiences of learning in educational institutions are different from those in other contexts. School learning is often de-contextualised, needs motivating, and tends to be individualistic, whereas learning out of school (and sometimes in school but out of classrooms) usually has 'real' context, comes more easily and is co-operative or shared. The exceptions to these generalisations are important for us to learn from. They regularly teach us that learning is more engaging when it relates to real problems and real contexts, and is more motivating when it engages the best of cooperation (as in the earlier section on *Effective learning in classrooms* – see page 29).

The consideration of context is increasingly important for schools, colleges and teachers, as research on learning is indicating that learning can often remain very tied to a context. In other words, the new knowledge that humans create can remain available to them only in the context where they created it. As educators, we make claims about the 'transfer' of learning, i.e. about its movement from one context to another. But studies have shown that transfer is not likely to occur unless a learner recognises that a new context has some similarity to the previous one in which knowledge was created.

Schools and colleges run the risk of becoming a specialised context of their own, and in the process creating too large a separation from other contexts of life and learning. In such circumstances the learning landscape has become fragmented and limited. Some students recognise this issue:

'I think we would learn better if we stayed at home and went out to see nature' (Kassandra).

Famous studies of Brazilian street-children showed that they were proficient in complex mathematical calculations on the street, but when the same calculations were asked of them in school they failed.

Within school, especially within the secondary school, different contexts for learning which are often described as a disadvantage of the school's organisation can be turned to an advantage – but only if we help pupils learn about them.

'Sometimes I learn by instruction when making food or construction structures. In maths they explain it to you or read it. In DT you learn by doing and watching. In ICT you learn by practising and explaining' (Ejsa)

Here, Ejsa has made a good start in identifying different demands and processes in different contexts. If she can build her profile of learning through all of them, and build the capacity to utilise the strategies appropriately for her goals in any context, she will become an effective and versatile learner.

13 SUPPORTING LEARNING

There are many different people who could play an important role in supporting a young person's learning: teachers, parents, learning support assistants, other family members, learning mentors and so on.

If it's really learning that we're supporting, then the message of this text brings three important areas to our notice.

1 To the extent that learners are learning through being taught (LBT), we can be supportive by trying to be clear and communicative in the purposes and processes of the learning we want them to undertake. It also means affirming the processes they use in their learning (to the extent that you can be aware of these).

   'When you have learned this you will be able to...'

   'I like the way that you...'

   'That's thinking along the right lines'

   However, this view is very limited by the fact that it is based on one-way communication.

2 Recognising that learners are making sense individually (LIS), we can be supportive by helping them elaborate this process. This involves inviting them to explain things to themselves and to others.

   'Talk me through how you...'

   'How did you get that bit?'

   'Could you tell Michelle how you did it?'

Similar approaches may help a learner move from a performance orientation to a learning orientation.

'What's gone well?'

'What's changed since you last tried it?'

'What did you enjoy most?'

'How did you manage that?'

'What's the toughest part?'

'What do you notice when things get tough?'

'I wonder what would happen if we tried it...'

3 Recognising that learners are in a social context creating knowledge as part of doing things with others (LBKO), we can be supportive by bringing the best of those others into the picture. This entails not seeing ourselves as the only source of help, and recognising that other sources may be more credible to that learner. It may also involve asking a learner to teach another – this is often an engaging challenge, and works against the idea that learners who 'need support' are full of deficits.

'Who would be best to help you with this?

'What might Y do in this situation?'

'How would you teach someone else?'

'How could you help X with their learning?'

Over recent decades, the term 'assessment' has been hi-jacked in our schools and colleges. The term derivates from the Latin word *assessere* which means 'to sit next to'. So, educational assessment is *to sit next to* someone to draw out their learning.

In our schools and colleges however, most people think 'testing' when someone says 'assessment'. Our pupils are the most tested in the world, and schools spend a massive £230 million a year on SATs and exams.

At worst, emphasis on tests can lead people to feel pressurised and to adopt strategic responses to what they do in school. This was expressed by one American commentator in the title of his book *'Learning to succeed in school – without really learning'*.

We want all our pupils to achieve well, so how can we avoid this worst-case scenario, without becoming an apologist for over-testing? The answer is that a focus on learning enhances performance (as elaborated on page 8).

So we need to reclaim the term 'assessment', and the headline phrase 'Assessment for learning' is sometimes used to indicate this. The core idea reflects the distinction in the diagram:

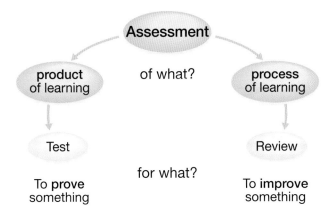

In current times, there are however some differences in how the term 'assessment for learning' is being used. Much depends on the meaning given to that key term – 'learning'. As earlier sections explained, three main views of learning can be identified, and each would lead to different processes of assessment.

View of learning	Observers take learning to be shown in:	Assessment in the form of:	Review in the form of:
1 Learning is being taught (LBT)	Responses to instruction: a 'show me' emphasis on visible and tangible 'knowledge' product	Timed, written tasks, with 'right answers' which reflect the instruction given	Practice tests and mock exams
2 Learning is individual sense-making (LIS)	Performances of understanding – 'explain to me', with more emphasis on spoken	Evidence of sense-making and meaning, as shown through dialogue	Individual reflection on the process of learning
3 Learning is building knowledge as part of doing things with others (LBKO)	Collaborative display resulting from authentic activities and acts of participation	Products such as a web of developing ideas and knowledge, a story or other form of collaborative account which shows the increasing complexity	Group reflection on the processes of action, collaboration, and dialogue

For some people, the idea of a learning-centred classroom is far-fetched, and given the trends of recent decades in UK classrooms (more whole-class teaching, more copying from the board), that may be understandable. But such classrooms do exist *here* in UK and *now* in the times we're in. For others, the idea of a learning-centred classroom is not an attractive proposition, because they view it as an extreme scenario ('pupils doing what they want') and this triggers their fears of 'losing control' which are based on old conceptions of the teacher's role.

Running a learning-centred classroom does not mean throwing everything out: it means shifting some of the focus from teaching to learning: it means addressing the same curriculum, but with a focus on learners and learning; it means giving attention to how the pupils are 'covering' the content, rather than the teacher. And it means helping pupils learn about their learning and thus be better prepared for the future.

Teachers who run learning-enriched classrooms have made a shift from the dominant model – instruction. They have resolved the tensions of the classroom in a new way, and have often made changes in the:

- balance of power – it has become more shared

- function of content – there is more focus on understanding

- role of the teacher – is more of an orchestrator

- responsibility for learning – is more with the pupils

- purpose and process of evaluation – is more to improve the classroom.

It would be wrong to overstate these changes, to the point of implying that they cannot happen in the climate which is current in the UK. Teachers sometimes say *'You couldn't do that – I have to prepare for the SATs',* and in so doing they revert to teacher-centred 'coverage' and 'delivery'. But learning-centred classrooms get better results, so we have to challenge the idea that the tests make us behave this way. Performance testing on its own does not create teacher-centred classrooms. Add the extra ingredient of judgement and fear, and this shifts the responsibility for learning – it is this ingredient which leads teachers to act in a more controlling way. In a context of pressure and compliance, this leads to a narrowed teacher repertoire and to teachers being described as 'risk-aversive'.

Teachers who operate learning-centred classrooms are those who know that things can be better, and are prepared to act according to their principles rather than according to their fears. They take what might seem to others to be risks, knowing that in education the biggest risk is not to take one!

Recognising that running a learning-centred classroom is a shift of emphasis and role, it is still possible to outline some of the practices. If we view learning as an individual making sense, they could include:

- an explicit focus on learning, for example in goals and products

- tasks framed in cognitive terms ('classify', 'analyse', 'predict')

- encouraging learners to plan and reflect before proceeding

- an explicit model of learning, for example 'Do-Review-Learn-Apply'

- learners generating their own questions and then attempting to answer them

- learners being asked to make sense (to themselves and to others) of what they meet

- promoting dialogue and collaboration

- reviewing learning, as opposed to performance

- a building-up of narrative about learning.

If we view learning as creating knowledge through doing things with others, practices could be:

- creating action together on shared tasks

- developing a classroom community goal, such as improving knowledge

- getting to know community members and the story each brings

- eliciting the questions brought to the theme

- jigsaw tasks which first separate and then re-combine a larger domain of study

- reciprocal teaching, class members teaching each other

- developing dialogue, to exchange ideas and understand others' thinking

- learning about learning and how the community best creates knowledge

- creating group goals for assessment

- building community governance, classroom reviews

- focusing on pro-social behaviour, development of trust, helping each other to learn.

Learning-centred schools and colleges share certain characteristics: staff relations are more collaborative, staff discussions often focus on learning, and pupil performance is higher. In current times such schools and colleges are fiercely independent: they are clear about their purposes and stick to them. They need to be strategic in the environment which has been created for schools and colleges, for example in having plenty of data available to justify their decisions to those who would challenge them.

Even through a device which was not designed for this purpose – the Ofsted framework for inspection – learning-enriched schools and colleges show up. In one primary school the word 'learn' was used 23 times in its inspection report, which concluded that in the under-privileged school, *'Pupils are highly motivated, independent learners'*.

Learning-enriched schools and colleges are not compliant places: the variety of learners and learning is welcomed and teaching has not been made routine. Indeed in learning-enriched schools and colleges when teachers are asked *'Do you ever have to break the rules in order to do what's best for pupils?'* the great majority say *'Yes'*. In many cases such schools and colleges are the ones who have gone beyond the routine prescriptions they are offered, and do so on the basis of their own evidence.

16 LEADING LEARNING

The three main views of learning which have recurred through this text can create very different views of what it means to 'lead learning'.

1. LEARNING IS BEING TAUGHT (LBT)

Leaders who see learning from this perspective are likely to:

- focus on teachers more than learners, especially their knowledge and 'competences'

- view the process of curriculum as one of delivering a body of knowledge

- value tangible products which are deemed to be easily measurable

- favour modes of assessment which are timed, summative performance tests, often through paper and pencil methods

- seek to improve performance by accelerating the pace at which learners get 'it' into their heads

- drive improvement through measurable indicators of product.

2. LEARNING IS INDIVIDUAL SENSE-MAKING (LIS)

Leaders who see learning from this perspective are likely to:

- focus on the way people make sense of their experiences

- view curriculum as addressing thought-demanding questions

- value processes which make learning a visible, central element: making reasoning public, thinking aloud together

- favour modes of assessment which ask people to explain to one another, give a reflective commentary

- seek to improve learning by slowing down the pace and focusing on quality of thinking

- drive improvement through indicators of quality learning experiences

- talk publicly about learning, and promote inquiry into learning

- support learning exchanges and peer teaching

- encourage others to do the above.

3. LEARNING IS BUILDING KNOWLEDGE AS PART OF DOING THINGS WITH OTHERS (LBKO)

Leaders who see learning from this perspective are likely to:

- focus on social and collaborative processes in teams and classes

- view curriculum as a process of building and testing knowledge

- view learning as a process of action and dialogue which leads to improvement in knowledge

- value processes which enhance collaborative and community outcomes

- favour modes of assessment which provide a community product

- seek to improve learning by enhancing collaborative enquiry and dialogue

- orchestrate improvement through indicators of the learning culture.

 Which of these do you recognise?

 In whatever leadership roles you have, (note that by leaders I do not mean bosses) which of these do you wish to develop further?

WHERE CAN I FIND OUT MORE?

The first and most important answer to this question is *'Ask your pupils'*. For insights into their learning experiences in the contexts that you and they know, there is no substitute. It may take a while to develop sophistication, but remember that it also improves communication, achievement and behaviour. If you have not yet started this process, then prepare yourself for some pleasant surprises.

The next important answer is also near at hand – your colleagues. If you can keep at bay the 'space invaders' identified at the start of this publication, then conversations about your own learning and about what you notice in pupils' learning will be rich and useful. If these are supported in collaborative encounters throughout the school, you really are part of a learning-enriched organisation.

Courses and projects can make a crucial contribution, especially as they bring together teachers from different organisational experiences. Much of what 'INSET' has become is the 'delivery' of a Government instruction agenda, so look for something which offers you a critical perspective, and really is about learning. Many LEAs have recognised this need and developed projects with a focus on learning.

Texts are regularly a good source of stories and ideas for you to relate to and adapt. These are ordered by the themes addressed.

- **Active learning**

Adams DM and Hamm M (1994), *New Designs for Teaching and Learning : promoting active learning in tomorrow's schools.* San Francisco: Jossey-Bass

Gagnon GW and Collay M (2001), *Designing for Learning: six elements in constructivist classrooms.* Thousand Oaks, CA: Corwin Press

- **Collaborative learning**

Slavin RE (1995), *Cooperative learning: theory, research, and practice* (2nd ed.). Boston: Allyn & Bacon.

Sharan S (Ed.) (1999), *Handbook of Cooperative Learning Methods.* Westport CN: Greenwood

- **Learner responsibility**

Areglado RJ, Bradley RC and Lane PS (1997), *Learning for Life: creating classrooms for self-directed learning.* Thousand Oaks CA: Corwin Press

Gibbons M (2002), *The Self-Directed Learning Handbook: challenging adolescent students to excel.* San Francisco: Jossey Bass

- **Learning about learning**

Watkins C (2001), *Learning about Learning Enhances Performance.* London: Institute of Education School Improvement Network (Research Matters series No 13)

Watkins C, Carnell E, Lodge C Wagner P and Whalley C (2000), *Learning about Learning: resources for supporting effective learning.* London: Routledge

- **Effective learning**

Carnell E and Lodge C (2002), *Supporting Effective Learning.* London: Paul Chapman

Watkins C, Carnell E, Lodge C, Wagner P and Whalley C (2002), *Effective Learning.* London: Institute of Education School Improvement Network (Research Matters series No 17)

- **Learning classrooms**

McCombs BL & Whisler JS (1997), *The Learner-centered Classroom and School: strategies for increasing student motivation and achievement.* San Francisco: Jossey-Bass

Weimer M (2002), *Learner Centered Teaching: five key changes to practice.* San Francisco: Jossey-Bass

Hughes M (1997), *Lessons are for Learning.* Stafford: Network Educational Press

- **Learning communities**

Wells G (Ed.) (2000), *Action, Talk, and Text: learning and teaching through inquiry.* New York: Teachers College Press

McEwan B (1999), *The Art of Classroom Management: effective practices for building equitable learning communities.* Prentice Hall

Rogoff B, Turkanis CG and Bartlett L (Ed.) (2001), *Learning Together: Children and Adults in a School Community.* Oxford University Press

- **Learning schools and colleges**

Clarke P (2000), *Learning Schools, Learning Systems.* London: Continuum

Senge PM, McCabe NH, Lucas T et al. (2000), *Schools That Learn.* New York: Doubleday

- **Learning theories**

Bransford J, Brown A and Cocking R (Ed.) (1999), *How People Learn: brain, mind, experience and school.* Washington DC: National Academy Press

Collins J, Harkin J and Nind M (2002), *Manifesto for Learning; fundamental principles.* London: Continuum

Hill WF (1997), *Learning: a survey of psychological interpretations.* New York: Longman

- **Assessment and feedback**

Askew S (Ed.) (2000), *Feedback for Learning.* London: Routledge

Carr M (2001), *Assessment in Early Childhood Settings: learning stories.* London: Paul Chapman

- **Other**

Bentley T (1998), *Learning Beyond the Classroom: education for a changing world.* London: Routledge

Bruner J (1996) *The Culture of Education.* Cambridge MA: Harvard University Press

Claxton G (2003), *Building Learning Power.* Westbury: TLO

Lambert NM and McCombs BL (Ed.) (1998), *How Students Learn: reforming schools through learner-centred education.* Washington DC: American Psychological Association

Nicholls JG and Thorkildsen TA (Ed.) (1995), *Reasons for Learning: expanding the conversation on student-teacher collaboration.* New York: Teachers College Press

Nystrand M and others (1997), *Opening Dialogue: understanding the dynamics of language and learning in the English classroom.* New York: Teachers College Press

Pollard A and Filer A (1996), *The Social World of Children's Learning: case studies of pupils from four to seven.* London: Cassell

Smith F (1998), *The Book of Learning and Forgetting,* New York. Teachers College Press

Vaill PB (1996), *Learning As A Way Of Being: strategies for survival in a world of permanent white water.* San Francisco: Jossey-Bass

Vaill PB (1998), *Spirited Leading and Learning: process wisdom for a new age.* San Francisco: Jossey-Bass

I hope your reading of this text may help you to be critically selective of what you find.

And finally, remember:

Those who bring learning to the lives of others cannot keep it from themselves.